Thoughts Of A Sinner

LESSONS. RHYMES. POEMS AND PRAYERS

WRITTEN BY: AL HAMILTON

Copyright © 2022

ISBN: 978-0-578-26218-5

Printed in U.S.A

Contents

Opening Scribe

What was initially born out of frustration, has now become an outlet with words. Eyes have grown tired, the body is emotionally drawn, and ears have gotten irritated.

The fear of failure and the desire of wanting more have inspired the writer to give the reader an inside look at the thoughts and perspectives of an honest sinner, with many tales of both young and old, growth and immaturity. The daily challenges of facing his own struggles fill these pages.

Given the writer's natural ability to express himself, being in tune with his feelings often came easy. However, what makes this piece of writing so unique, is the boldness within the lines, written in pure honesty, and packed with a fierce punch of pain.

The author has attempted to find his own deliverance. It is the writer's belief that by unveiling his truths, every reader will be gifted the opportunity to become vulnerable, helping all readers find their own truths.

CH Trauma

I might fade to black if I can push Perms back,
Straighten out a whole wig, under that baseball cap.
All facts, no lying if I'm lying, I'm flying,
My feet planted in the soil, I've been labeled a tyrant,
My mind was stuck on violence, with so much anger and aggression.
There was nothing they could say to me,
I was headed for the grave, if I was lucky, penitentiary,
It never really bothered me, suspended almost constantly.
My teachers didn't rock with me; they stuck me in Special Ed,
Some treated me like I was stupid, thought my mind was dead,
I used to ride that little school bus; I used to duck my head,
People laughed at my clothes, when I was prescribed the meds,
I started to feel different, that Ritalin had me trippin',
So, I quit that,
Started selling pills, like they was Kit Kats.
Nobody ever listened to me, couldn't get them to pay attention,
I was caught in the midst,
I was trying to figure it out, but I never had an outlet,
Hung around in the streets, but didn't want to pump bricks,
Got my hands on a gun, I tried to shoot, but I missed,
Seen a lot, and done a lot, ain't proud of none it,
But this is only page one,
It's still some more that comes with this.

Intentional Prayer

Father God, I come to you right now in the name of your son, Jesus.

I am asking that you hear me as I communicate with you today. If it shall be in your will, I am asking that you direct my heart and prepare me for this journey.

Live in me and help me to lessen myself and find increase in you.

Today I ask that you reveal your purpose in my life.

Father, you know me better than I know myself.

You have seen all my flaws, and you are the strength to my pain.

My weakness is your joy; you know my passion along with my shortcomings.

Father, it is in you that I seek rest.

It is not my will that I am seeking, but yours.

Today I am intentional about my prayer.

I am requesting that you give me the vision to see and an understanding to accept my purpose within this union.

Abba Father, Amen.

Wash and Rinse

Life isn't about taking the easy route.

It's every bit of how you navigate its terrain.

Life is a beautiful journey; it's about learning lessons and gathering information.

Life is about teaching and sacrificing, experiencing new environments, and gaining knowledge while you explore.

Every situation in life brings about a different degree of lessons.

Either it teaches you how to become something,
Or you're teaching someone else how to evolve into something.

Either way, life is about breaking down and building up.

This is what the cycle of life is all about.

The wash and the rinse,
Growth and elevation, creating and recreating.

The Ladder

I identify with the struggle,

I became one with my pain.

I've been labeled the abuser,

I don't mind standing toe to toe in the ring.

I have chosen not to let it bother me.

I am choosing destiny over constraint.

I intentionally choose to be positive,

Rather than the negativity that attacks my brain.

Right now, I'm choosing to grow up.

This is the best chance for me to seek change!

When you've been accustomed to having things, certain things just don't move you anymore.

Certain words, people, and situations no longer have the same shock value that they used to.

It's okay to set a standard for things you've moved away from.

It's perfectly okay to tell people, "No!"

You have a right to choose what you will and what you won't accept in life.

Do not be ashamed of breaking the mold; expand your vision and lay the foundation.

It's your life, execute, and be satisfied with the results.

Be Dangerous!

The Come Up

Play broke until the time is right,
Trends come around every year.
You want to be the wave, not ride one,
Waves last forever.
Even though moments may be epic,
They're never long-lived.
The slow grind wins every time.
It's okay to have a date with the moon; the goal is to sleep with the sun!
Small investments are major improvements.
Your foundation is the most important part of your future,
Be mindful of the people that surround you!
Some deals are too good to pass up,
And that's why relationships matter.
Every moment should count for something,
Your timing is everything.
The most important key of opportunity,
Is to only purchase when necessary.
Simplicity sells!

A Hint of Me

Just a lost soul trying to find peace
Just a lost soul trying to find me
Kind of humble
A little loud
I don't know about meek
My apologies if I offend you
But I can only be me

The Pressure

You overcome, then you achieve
And then you overcome a little more
Some much hostility and restraint
As you hit the front door
Be ready for war, full armor on
You must protect your chest
Dressed in your army suit
Strapped with a kevlar vest
But when stress is the opposition
Then it's the mind that needs rest
There's no protection in the world
That can protect you from that
Got your mind going in circles
And your thoughts steady pacing
Anxiety running a marathon
But the body not racing
Scared to look yourself in the mirror
Don't know what you might be facing
Candyman in your dreams
And you can't escape, Jason
No amount of money can ever free you from that
But what's inside of you
That's the fight in you
It's a must to Stand Up
Come Out
And illuminate the light in you

Just Me

Constantly and consistently
I'm my worst enemy
I ask questions of others
Hoping that they might get it
An opportunity to show me
Something to ease my pain
Something that I inflicted
Nothing I want to deal with
But inevitably, it can't be
The mission is cut short
The journey becomes frustrating
My goal is never fulfilled
So onward I press
In search to find myself
As I challenge my own standards
I seek to find help
Relentlessly, I search
Hoping there's a better tomorrow
Optimism is an attribute, but my confidence is still shaky
So, I smile, and I hide
A skill that was never given, one that I stole from
Because I had to survive
Every day my mind wonders
Creativity, she keeps calling me
Fighting back the old me
While molding who I am trying to be

A Mirror of Me

Think strategically and find enough strength to push through.

Be mindful of your emotions while managing each scenario.

Think about your reaction; the opportunity cost could be enormous.

Think *Me, Myself, and I...*

Set the example, instead of being made one.

All your faults, and all your shortcomings,

They will be judged by others, but only if given the opportunity to.

Learn to analyze yourself.

Critique and criticize your own behavior,

Before someone else is allowed to.

A Prayer of Cleansing

Dear Heavenly Father,

In your hands, I place my life. Fully and faithfully, I am trusting you that your will be done. I release all control as I honor your decrees. I ask that you guide and order my steps as I start fresh, on a new path today.

You are my father, and I am your child. From this moment on, I vow to seek your kingdom. Please cleanse my heart and create in me a new image and a cleaner version that we both may be proud of.

Father God, help me to forgive things of the past and cover me with the full armor of the holy spirit.

Retrain me, and teach me how to walk with you in the light.

Abba Father, Amen.

Lesson in Leadership

You may not always agree with leadership.

But soon, you will learn to appreciate the lessons of leadership, especially when it becomes your turn to lead.

Correction and Corrective Action is not always as it seems; it's not always based on wrongdoing.

Often, it's about education and what you can improve upon.

Lesson:

If you want to be a good leader, you must first learn to be an extraordinary follower.

Moral Compass

Beyond words and actions, the mere understanding of right and wrong.

Possessing the ability to have respect for another without being held accountable.

To speak and to stand, to consider the significance of life and death.

A person's integrity allows for them to stretch beyond themselves.

To rationalize what lies beneath.

The soul of a person, not the skin color, is where the value must lie.

The soul of an individual is far greater in return, than any stocks or bond could ever be.

A moral compass cannot be traded for cheap; it cannot be altered or diminished, nor should anyone suggest trying to devalue it, with the replacement of monetary gain.

Lesson:

Outside of any material items that you own and any amount of money that you have in the bank account, you are who you are!

When you leave here (wherever you are geographically on earth), your legacy is what you leave behind.

Capacity

It doesn't matter how educated a person is

How well-liked a person may be

Or how nice they are to you

You cannot continue to be in the company of individuals with a small mind

And a lack of vision

Restricted thinkers will only stifle your growth

Your expansion is largely based on the type of company you keep

Brand Recognition

The world has all the makings of what you would expect for it to be, to enjoy your life in such a beautiful place. However, if you want to assure yourself of the beauty that comes with the scenery, there are two things that you must get understood first.

The first is knowing who you are, and the second is knowing where you fit within the dynamics of the universe. While those two may seem simple, discovery along life's journey may cause confusion.

The universe has its own way of shaping the minds of those who struggle with the concept of owning their identity. Many individuals are easily captured on the canvas, but they are also consumed with comparisons.

Comparing one good to another is sometimes necessary, but only when trying to discover texture and quality. It is wise to realize that you are a person, an actual human being.

Therefore, you are someone who was created perfectly in your own image and likeness. There are no imitations of you; there is no imagination needed.

You are a true-to-life rare breed, a one of one.

It is essential that you find confidence in who you are.

Embrace your uniqueness. Allow your light to glow and illuminate the world around you.

There is no need to compare your brand to another brand. If you find yourself wanting to be like another person, I urge you to ask yourself a question.

Why?

What is the purpose of having your own brand if your only concern is being alike, sounding alike, looking alike, and doing what someone else does?

Does that not defeat the purpose of your exceptional qualities?

In fact, it does!

Be at peace with who you are.

Confront the social norms by being distinct in your actions.

Be the brand that you know you can trust.

Your own!

I'D Rather

Show you my love, than hate you for nothing
Give you a hug, than turn my back on you
Wish you success, rather than see you fail
Give you my heart, than see you in pain

I'd rather live in peace, with joy all around me
Instead of live among my enemies in constant conflict
I'd rather lift you up, than try to tear you down

I would rather die like a man, instead of begging on my knees
Because that isn't the life that God has promised to me
I'd rather smile and be happy, and live life with the bros
Marry a beautiful wife, have some kids, and grow old

A Wise Mind Prayed

Let us not blame those that oppose us.
But with dignity,
We must treat them with the same courtesy that has been extended unto us.

Let's not be angered by those that despise us,
Instead, teach us to be grateful.

Teach us to be fulfilled for such a gesture, It is a grand gesture,
To have someone to think of you,
That they might position you in the midst of their thoughts.

With grace,
Teach us to show love and support to those that speak out against you.
For we too, are flawed, bathing in a pool of our own confusion and
mistakes.

Father teach us to be grateful,
And to forever be humble.

Never too proud, boastful, filled with envy, or hatred.

A sober spirit knows better than to think so highly of themselves,
one must always be a willing participant to the glory of God.

Now let us bow our heads, offer up, and extend our hands,
in search of our own forgiveness.

Abba Father, Amen.

Broken

I'm not afraid of what is or what may come to be.

But what I am afraid of is wondering.

I hate overthinking!

I often ask myself, did you give it everything you had?

Were you in the correct place?

Did you meet the quality of your expectations, and the standards set before you?

Did you talk too much?

Was there anyone who might've been offended?

And what about your delivery? Were you ever too harsh to anyone?

These are the things that I consistently ask myself.

I do my best to always maintain a winning mentality, however, my attitude is something that I constantly struggle with.

Past traumas have forced me to become more self-aware, and to be more considerate of others.

Unfortunately, this has become a daunting task.

For me, success is my greatest escape.

However, winning just isn't good enough for me anymore.

There's no solace in winning, and I can't find that same desire to succeed that I once had.

Proving others wrong no longer makes me feel complete.

I have this exigent desire for wanting more, and I can't control it.

My eagerness to succeed is becoming unrealistic.

And now I'm struggling to find that ultimate happy place.

From the looks of it, I guess it's safe to say that I'm broken.

C.T.F.

If I could have saved bro life, I would have done it twice already

We were high off the life, trying to make it through them nights

Escaped a situation or two, thank God that we made it through

I wonder if they really knew, everything we been through

Broke a couple dice games, just to play AAU

Big pots, we bet it all

Money good when it's off the wall

The streets really raised us; your mama really prayed for us

When class was still in session, we was trying to get our grades up

Though times really made us, a hater couldn't fade us

An uphill battle, I won't stop until we make it up

Real Ain't Real

"Keep It Real"

Is one of the most overused phrases there is

Fraudulent people use it all the time

Keeping it 100 creates a false narrative

Because most who use it, they don't even keep it 10 percent of 100 with themselves

Peep game

Karma is like a red ant

She burns like hell when she bites

Learn not to be so real with others

That you become bogus with yourself

Lesson:

There are far too many people in this world competing for the spotlight and the approval of others. Meanwhile, they strive to keep it real with everybody else; they often misuse and abuse the most important aspect of life… SELF.

Is worth nothing. But it will cost you everything!

Lesson:

Do not be mistaken. Time is worth something. But it is all about what you are willing to pay for it. Unlike fuel, you cannot go into the gas station and ask for twenty dollars on pump five.

However, if you are not careful, and you abuse the free time given, whatever goals you are trying to accomplish; later it is going to cost you a lot more.

And you can bet whatever dollar amount you want. I can assure you; it is going to be a whole lot more than the twenty dollars you tried to put on pump five.

Struggling

There's a lot of animosity behind those jokes
And a lot of tears behind those smiles
It's more pain than pleasure when you see that hard work
Don't believe everything you see on the surface
People are struggling on the inside
And keeping busy is the motivation
That's the only way to suppress the truth
Because everybody's struggling with something

Somebody's Baby

No matter the age, race, gender, or origin, we are all somebody's baby.
We may have come into this world at contrasting times, at various
places, with different beliefs and different upbringings.

But the facts are the facts; we are all somebody's baby.

You may have survived the struggles of a tough neighborhood and born
into poverty.
You may also be the person with little adversity and now thriving in your
career.
But again, I say this; you are still somebody's baby.
It does not matter if you came from a broken home, if you were abused
as a child, and still misunderstood as an adult.

You are still somebody's baby.

So, here is my point because you are somebody.

You deserve the right to be treated as somebody.
Ill-prepared and uneducated; you are still somebody's baby.
Poor, broke, and homeless, you are still somebody's baby.

This world and this society need to keep that in mind; you are still
somebody's baby.
A token of love should be the standard of having respect for each other.
Life needs to have a common balance that keeps the universe in working order.

Because at the end of the day, you are still somebody's baby.

Making a New Thing

I get it; we all get scared in life. New experiences and new opportunities bring about changes. An even though change is good, change can sometimes leave you with an incredibly awkward feeling.

However, what we all must keep in mind is that change is a normal part of life. Change is a natural part of the evolution process; change is supposed to happen. Change is like working out; it stretches us and forces us to grow stronger.

And yes, I know what you're thinking. Is it normal to question yourself while you are in transition? Yes, it's normal. Every transitional stage is going to offer a new component, with various challenges ahead.

In fact, to be rather honest, something might be wrong with you if you didn't stop to question yourself. All those questions like, should I stay, or should I go, do I leave, and what will happen once I do leave—those are all normal thoughts and questions that anyone should ask.

While I am not an expert in the matter of psychology, what I have noticed in my own situations is this: Overthinking is where the problem lies.

It's the simple questions that have the greatest impact on your mental process.

In my opinion, there are two ways to think about the unknown. One side of it is extremely scary, and the other side of it is exciting, adventurous, and new. Just like any other area of your life, you had to transition into that space. In the beginning, it was the unknown that you first experienced.

No matter how simple it was, you transitioned into it. You fed yourself for the first time, and then you learned how to walk as you took your first steps.

We all try to do our best when changing from one stage to the next. But regardless of your transition, here is what I want to leave you with.

Lesson:

No matter how hard the road gets in your transitioning phase, always remember that there lies another opportunity for you to make and create a bunch of new memories along the way.

A Champion's Prayer

Originally written at 2:05am on 3/24/2018

Dear Lord,

I come to you today on bending knees, with my arms open wide.

Father, I ask in Jesus' name that you keep us, that you lead us, and that you heal us.

Father, I pray right now that your will be done.

Whatever you see fit for us, I pray that you have your way. I pray that our hearts and minds be fixed upon you.

Father, let us not forget why we are here.

Help us to walk in the light and live out our purpose for you.

Today is a purposeful prayer, and I pray that we all continue to become the servants that you have created and designed for us to be.

And if not now, then tomorrow, and if not then, then in the future.

Of all these things, I ask in the mighty name of your son Jesus...

Abba Father, Amen.

Time Is of The Essence

Borrowed time is one the greatest assets you'll ever encounter. It's more valuable than property, and more consistent than casino chips.

The unfortunate deal with borrowed time, it is going to run out.

And the very second that it does, it's gone.

Therefore, it is with great importance that you understand your responsibilities.

You've got to find which is the most efficient and effective way to garnish a return on your investment.

Time…

This isn't an occasion when you want to be sloppy. Focus and attention to detail are high priorities at the moment. Don't take your hands off the wheel and lose control.

EXECUTE, EXECUTE, EXECUTE!

Do not second guess yourself.

Take pride in who you are and the abilities that you have at your disposal.

Now is your greatest opportunity to cash in and win big. You have nothing at stake when you play with borrowed time; it's house money.

Maximize your situation!

Believe in the power of You!

You are your greatest asset!

Take advantage while you still can.

Because time is of the essence.

Cold Dark Room

You can tell the people whatever you want to, but the truth of the matter is this,
You cannot escape the truth which lies inside of you.

When you are sitting alone in that cold dark room, you cannot lie to you.
You'll be forced to face your fears and deal with the reality of you.

All alone with no one to talk to, the cold and lonely truth will reveal itself.
And that is when your issues become real.

You won't be able to run anymore, and you won't be able to hide.

It's at that moment that you will know; now is the time that I must face the truth and walk into the darkness of honesty.

The truth sometimes can be cold, rotten, and mean,
However, it'll be the truth in the end that makes you better and not bitter.

The reward of that cold dark room will have served its purpose.

Isolation brings about strength; your strength will help you face the facts and learn to be okay with them.

Lesson:

Always remember: Never let the outside world change you from being who you are.
If you ever get lost, the truth will forever be with you…
In your cold dark room…

Her

I needed a coaster for my pain
So, I shared my love with a napkin
Poured my tears into a glass
And drank it before she could see it
I let the pain bleed through
It was too messy for her to read it

Rough Patches

Be thankful for fresh starts and new beginnings

There is an abundance of surprises for you on the other side

Be not misled by your own shallow thinking

Comfort yourself, by taming your emotions and becoming one with your inner you

I urge you to push beyond the misconception of what you think God's love is

Confront your fears, by embracing the challenging moments

Just keep believing

Because the only work that matters, is the work that you haven't completed yet

The power of his love is magnanimous, tested, tried, and sustained

The reward has already been given to you

The work that you are suspecting God to complete

It has already been done for you

Know that his deed is greater than the gift that you seek

Your blessing has already been shipped out

Priority Delivery

It is now your job to follow through on the assignment

God is patiently waiting for you to arrive

Catch up

Overcompensating

Don't do it.
Stop overcompensating
For things and people that do not deserve your attention.
Don't do it,
The risk isn't worth it.
And neither are the people who you are adjusting for.
Don't do it,
You'll hate yourself for it later.
And you'll regret it too.
Don't overcompensate,
Just don't do it!

The Sunken Place

You left me when I needed you. You lied to me!
We took an oath together; said we would always be honest.
And to tell you the truth, I'll never forget it,
When things changed between us, a foggy day in October.
You dissed me and left me, with a fuckin' cold shoulder.
So, I returned you the money, and my heart got colder,
And just for a second, I knew, that I found it,
Back in my commonplace,
You know that place that I told you,
Where I've never wanted to revisit,
It's the place in my life, where I hide my pain in it.
It's a place that I've known; it feels just like home,
That place when strategy strikes, where nothing else even matters,
When the odds are on high, and it's always stacked against me,
It's never where I want to be, but it feels so familiar,
I hate it here, but I'm comfortable too,
It kind of feels weird, but I just can't move.

Lesson:

Try stretching yourself today; find out what loving you is all about. Because trying to love someone else is hard, and it is not an easy thing to do, especially without the proper tools. Rejection is never an easy thing to deal with. The recovery process is tough, it's weird, and it's never a comfortable situation. But regardless of your pain and how uncomfortable it makes you feel, learning to be vulnerable and embracing those feelings inside you has major advantages.

A Personal Conversation

Part 1

Self: Yo, AL!

AL: What up, Self?

Self: AL, baby, you trippin' again!

AL: What you mean? How, Self?

Self: AL, you're letting other people's feelings cloud your vision. I need you to snap out of it!

AL: Man, cut it! How you figure that?

Self: AL, listen to me, baby. You know I know you!

AL: Self, I hear you talking. But do you hear yourself, though, you're starting sound crazy.

Self: AL!!!

AL: What up, Self?!

Self: Be honest with me; tell me you don't feel that?

AL: What are you talking about, Self? What am I supposed to feel?

Self: The energy! Tell me you don't feel it…?

AL: I do…

Self: See, that's the shit I'm talking about.

Self: You're letting them control you! They're dumbing that bad juju on you, and now you're losing focus again!

Self: You've gotta snap out it. We've been here before. And we don't have time for this…

AL: I feel you, Self… I feel you.

Self: I know you do. But are you hearing me?

Self: Listen to me, dawg… We don't have time for this!

AL: Trust me; I got you… I'm 100 percent with you…

Lesson:

Sometimes it's not about how many licensed professionals you talk to. You can talk to as many people as you like, but none of them know you like you know yourself. And believe it or not, a conversation with yourself is all it takes. Honesty is the key, and you can't hide from you... So why not have a conversation? You got somewhere to go?

The Game

"I Think I Love Her"

I don't want to stress her; I want to encourage her.
I don't want to hate her; I want to love her.

We both have hurt, and I can feel it inside, but it's so frustrating trying to get her to explain it to me.
How is it fair to me when I've been open from the start? Why do I have to put in all the work?

Why won't she just let me in? This is too complicated; why won't she let me be great?

How did it come to this?

It was all good just a week ago. At one point, we were growing, playing together, praying together, and in connection every day.

And then it all changed... I don't understand what happened...

God, what did I do? I don't understand... Where did we go wrong?
And how did everything change so quickly?
What is it? Is it me? Was it something I did?

How is it that we have such amazing chemistry, and then our balance be off?

Father, if you showed it to me, how can we not be right for each other?

You gave me the insight. Is my timing off?

I'm not trying to question you, but I am asking for clarification.
Please help me understand it! What is it that you want from me?

Father, I want to trust you; I really do. But I've been calling your line,
and I still can't reach you.

I'm fighting hard to keep my composure, but I'm nervous of losing
again.
And I don't know if I can stand another heartbreak.
I think I love her, The Game...

I Told You So

Don't call me and don't talk to me,

I'm not listening no more!

I hate to have to tell you, but I told you so.

I tried to tell you before it happened,

But you wouldn't listen to me.

You thought you knew it better than I did, and you listen to them.

So now I'm being quiet; I'm not saying nothing else.

I'm tired of talking, because I'm only talking for my health,

And what's the use of doing that when I'm just talking to myself...

A Prayer for You

Dear Brothers and Sisters
May the love of our Father in heaven
Keep you and cover you today
May this prayer find you in perfect peace
Granting you the ultimate grace and security
To be fulfilled and full
Overflowing
In both joy and favor
God is love

Abba Father, Amen!

Deflection

Stop submitting to the critiques and opinions of outside noise
They haven't experienced the disarray that you've survived
You are exceptionally designed, formed in a mold that is unbreakable
Gifted with incredible abilities

Caution yourself that you keep your sacred space clear of undesirable energies
If allowed, people will care for you and mistreat you at the same time
Manipulation is a beautiful game
Be not surprised when those closest to you leave you
Especially when you need them the most

Everyone has a separate hand in the pot
It can be quite mystifying for others to see what you see
Your vision is your vision, and your dreams are your own

Unconditional

Inspire by Adonis "Don Don" Jenkins

Too smooth homie, now you stuck in a box

So, I'm praying for a ghetto (up in heaven) just in case it's not

Know you gotta grind hard, go, and hit that block

Better holler at me now, might not catch me later

Trying to get up, get out, and go catch this paper

Damn you, dog, that was something of the essence

I'm listening to the teacher, but I can't learn his lessons

Fuck a Smith and Wesson, homie how do I live

I know you bust your fuckin' ass to take care of ya kids

As I'm staring at this man like, that's what it is

If I could be anything, I'd be like this

Fuck a cold bottle, let's pop this Chris(tal)

I bet your damn car don't run like this

20-inch white walls, blue candy 'bout to fall

Shit, we bout to blow up like, Colione

Yeah, that's me, dog, I'm carrying on

Helpless

If I could offer her the gift

I could get over the curse

Trying to balance out her pain, is getting heavy, and it hurts

I can see it in her eyes, too many tears she cried

She keeps telling me it's nothing; I don't know why she keeps lying

Thinking I don't know about it, like I haven't been in the back

Listening to them stories, trying to grow up 'round that

They were big; I was small

I was little; they were tall

My little body filled with anger

I was trying to finish them off

But I was helpless

Divine Order

When God tells you to move, it's time to move!
From one place to another, from an old place to a new place, honor his direction.
The most common habit that we all struggle with is wondering "what if" and trying to look back.
That's a normal part of the change process but trust the decision you've made; you can't go back.

Straddling the fence will only lead you on a destructive path, hence the reason why you were given the direction in the first place.

Pay attention to the signs and listen intently for *your* next direction.

Disconnecting from what appears to be normal has its own set of trails. Therefore, think it not unusual when you start to experience some discomfort in the initial stages of your separation.

Hopefully, in the end, you'll understand why a separation was necessary.

The longer you reject the direction appointed to you, the more damage you ultimately do to yourself.
When you leave, leave completely! And whatever gets left behind, it should stay behind. Don't stress about, it can be replaced.

Focus on maximizing what you have, and double down on trusting God's plan for your life!
Once you make the decision to jump, go with both feet in; your faith will sustain you in the midst of the storm.

You may not realize it at that very moment, but the strength of your faith is working at a premium during this time.

Trust the transition! Do not lose hope when things seem to look bleak.

Lock in and stay focused. Because rest assured, you will be tested; the ride is going to get bumpy but hold on tight.

The stage is set, and a new adventure is forthcoming ahead!

Deflection

Part 2

You are your own living testimony
Somebody somewhere is going to need your story
You do not have time to pause
And give attention to criticisms and critiques
Your plan and paths are laid out in front of you
You are on an assignment
You mustn't stop now
Please keep going
And run your race

All for You

So much pleasure in my pain, it gotta be working
If I can make my mother proud, it'll all be worth it
Just to see my mother smile, you know that I'm working
Top tier while I'm here, no short circuits
I came a mighty long way from that kid in bricks
Shout out to Shady Side, baby, I'm loving that shit
To see the hood giving back, keep reppin' that shit
And I gotta do what I do to stay relevant too
I hear the voices of lost souls; they haunting me, dude
And Colione, no matter what, Ima make you proud
Every time I talk to Petey, I hug him, and I smile
I'm writing this book for my sister, so she can see how
Anything is possible, once you figure it out
A wild soldier child, I'm making rounds
For the ghetto boys and girls, who can't figure it out
No need to worry, cause I'm here
I'm holding it down
For all the people in my town, just look at me now
I'm about to rewrite history, and rename the town

A Victim's Prayer

Father,

I've been a victim of my own shit, struggling at my own risk
I heard if you want to be a boss, it's some sacrifices you need to make

I grew up so fast, I never learned how to laugh
I walked around angry; everyone was always blaming me

Why they always hate on me when I give it up faithfully
My family still in the hood, and I hate going back
My mama and my sister still in the projects
And I try to lend a hand; I'm supposed to be the strongest

But I'd rather be a loner, you know, sit by myself, stay away, off in the
corner

The bastard child of the family, I can tell they envy me

They hate it when I'm around, regardless of how much I've grown
It's the old shit that comes out; I'm steadily fighting demons
In tune with my soul, on the inside, I be screaming
On my back every night, it's so hard not to cry
I talk to God every day, asking him to ease the pain

Detach me from these shackles, and let me break out these chains
They've been holding me back, and I'm just trying to move further
Away from this shit, but it just keeps pulling me

I don't know what else to do, that's why I'm writing out my thoughts
I'm sending my prayers to you, but so far, I feel lost

I don't know if I'm even comfortable; I'm losing my grip
When it comes to transparency, having you as my friend

It's kind of hard to open up, trust, and let people in

I feel like I'm the safest bet, and I'm not losing again

Amen.

As Real as It Gets

Not for all the fanfare, I don't care

I don't really need it,

Not concerned if you salute me, you can leave me where you see me,

No longer are you free to roam with lofty expectations,

How can you ever expect the same love when you don't reciprocate it?

Stop lying to yourself; you know that none of it's true

Old thoughts of truth and love, even honesty too

Emotionally, I'm not relevant, not even to you.

This world artificial, and it's bogusly drawn,

It lacks the truth in authenticity, and now my heart has been scorn.

Big Homies

Be open with your little homies

Don't hide the game from 'em

Teach me what they need to know, or get away from 'em

Don't take advantage of 'em

Because you're trying to gain something

That ain't real shit; that's not what big homies do

You look like a lame for that, the owl and the sucker too

If you do underhanded shit, its gonna boomerang back to you

So don't get to complaining

And start talking about what somebody else did to you

Big homies play it smooth, never weird, and unusual

It ain't never cool to charge a homie, on something you get for free

If your little homie down bad, help him to his feet

Teach him how to fish, so he can learn how to eat

Because that's the role you accepted, once you became the OG

Lesson:

Don't play yourself. Big homie to little homie, little homie to big homie. Respect each other or get away from each other. If you can't speak to each other in a civil manner, there's no love there, especially when it comes to mistakes and misunderstandings.

Big Dreams

But I haven't woke up yet
Still wishing on a star
But I haven't seen one yet
Scared if I wake up
I won't reach my best
So, I'm dreaming all night
Until I run out of breath
And when the morning comes
I wanna see the morning sun
Screaming, *hallelujah*
The day has just begun

Cry Baby, Cry

Ms. Katie, my lady

The golden things you used to tell us

If you gonna cry, let me get some money for them tears

You used to put a mason jar under our eyes

And instantly, the tears would stop

And suddenly disappear

We'd all start smiling, and the laughter filled the air

And as much as we tried

Staying mad, we couldn't do it

And you knew it, that's just how much you cared

We'd act and play tough

And say, Granny, get outta here

Then you'd smile and show your dentures

At that moment, we had enough

You would always find a way

To make us laugh and cheer us up

And your smile was infectious

It was only the simple stuff

What I wouldn't give for more of your love

Emotional Maturity

Such an extremist, I promise you, I take it to the max

No time for hesitation, but I need time to relax

Once I hear about it, that's it, I'm flipping, it's off rip

But how embarrassing of me, to completely lose my cool

So uncontrollable, to let you play me like a flute

The fool in me, is to be controlled by a mood

Every time the wind blows, it changes the tempo

Went from lukewarm to timber, and the time didn't change

Went from super happy then, and now you see the rage on my face

I think it's time that I mature; I need to heal from within

Not an advocate of looseness, I view it being foolish

How you expect to be a boss, and people thinking you clueless

You trying to win the crowd, you can't play them people like that

Show respect to the real; you know it's coming right back

Loyalists pick up the phone, and get a call right back

You got to be solid in your thoughts, even stronger with your movements

Once you have your mindset, you got to stick to it and pursue it

Keep your head above water, until you see yourself through it

Humble Prayer

Father God,

I call upon your name right now. I am yet seeking the kingdom once again.
I am asking for your favor to fall upon me.
Impart in me your wisdom; give me the guidance and the mental capacity to understand where I am right now.

I know you're in this place because I feel your presence surrounding me.
I've witnessed you in many ways during this life of mine, and I acknowledge you in every moment.

But if I'm truly being honest, my faith is shaken right now, and I've lost trust in you.
Lord, you know my heart, and you know my desires.
I just want to be great at something.
I just want to be a better person than who I used to be.

With so many ups and downs in life, I'm tired of the roller coaster.
I'm stressed, and I'm ready to get off this ride.

Father, you know my heart; in it, is the consistency that I seek.
I need your love! And I need you more now than I ever have before!

I confess; I need the blood of Christ to come forth in my life, and to flow like the rushing waters.

I am not ashamed to call out: Abba Father!

To let you know that I seek healing, wisdom, and peace,

But most of all, I only want what you have prepared for me.

In Jesus name, I pray,

Abba Father, Amen...

Eyes Wide Open

I stumbled upon you, and I didn't even try to
One hundred percent fact, I can't even lie to you
Thought you were truly genuine, now you not even dog food
Got no reason to hate, but I don't want to talk to you
Learned a lot of lessons in a short amount of time
Perspective is what you make it, and the grind is the grind
Eyes wide open, it's only a matter of time
Never focused on what you got because none of it mine
I'm a man in the flesh, even stronger in the spirit
You won't believe me when I tell you, but it's the truth once you hear it
You stand confident away, but it's the fear when you near it
Don't need no validation, or any guest appearances
I'm headed to the top, without security clearances

You are Y

Always remember your Y
Your reason for doing what You do
Remember the time that You invested
Your family's sacrifices

You are the Y
Never forget about You

Your shortcomings, Your downfalls
Your lonely nights and your alone times
All your empty feelings, and all that You had to endure
Your struggles and Your grind
All those hard times You had to face alone

Remember when You fell,
And what You had to do to get back on Your feet
Never forget about You

You are the reason Y

What I Taught You

If you haven't learned anything from me, hopefully, you've learned to always be yourself.

To think as a leader, to develop and live as leaders do.

In my opinion, a true leader listens to others, and hears what needs to be said,

But is wise enough to discern between what is real and what is not.

In some instances, a leader must be bold enough to disagree,

And disregard what others think about you.

The mark of a true leader is identity,

There is nothing wrong with taking pride in being your own person.

Individuality,

To stand alone is a great honor,

Because it allows you the space and opportunity to learn and to grow.

However, there is a downside to being alone,

Leadership can be a thankless position.

In moments when you find yourself at odds with the outside world,

That's when prioritizing takes place,

Focus on your responsibilities.

Your time becomes more valuable in these moments.

What you put energy into, reflects how you prioritize your time.

You cannot afford to be reckless right now. So, get a firm grip on your attitude.

A concentrated effort breeds consistency in areas where you lack strength.

Humility *sustains* the *appreciation* from inflexible circumstances.

Empty Dreams and Broken Promises

As a child, I had so many dreams of becoming successful.
But unfortunately, there always seemed to be someone around me
making a promise that they couldn't keep.
Some may have been out of their control,
However, those unlikely results played a significant part in emptiness
growing up.
I needed to find my own strength to overcome; therefore, I was forced to
move along.
No matter the situation, or the obstacle,
I had to keep going.
Often stressing about the lies that were told on life,
People played a lot of games; I was treated as a pawn,
Family stole my inheritance; I struggled to persevere,
I wasn't of importance; people really didn't care,
Constantly worrying about my future and those things that never came
to pass.
Furiously upset at those who stole my dreams,
I learned to camouflage my pain,
It was a beautifully painted picture; I did it just to save face,
Didn't want to expose the figure. I found power in my brokenness.
I admit, it took me a long time to be honest.
My anger was my motivation, trying to stay strong and not feel hatred,
To love willingly, even though they stole my sincerity,
To love you unconditionally, after you lied and looked at me,
I know too much truth that I'm not willing to prove,
If I pondered on these empty things, the drama it would bring,
Never will I ever let it, make me less than what I am.
Empty dreams and broken promises, I leave it in God's hands...

Let Go of My Ego

I'm down for the culture, and I love us too. And yes, I'm still going to be me. I'm still going to speak my mind, right, wrong, or indifferently...

I'm also going to tell you the truth. Because I realize, that is what's needed from me. And because people value what I have to say. I understand that it's more than just the message, it's the tone in my delivery.

Therefore, we must get to a place where understanding is a common ground. Getting an understanding is far more significant than what we are "trying" to say.

Overall, what we must acknowledge, regardless of our status and our position, no matter the leverage you have, remaining humble is of the highest! Your ego is not more important than the survival of our youth.

Nobody cares about your feelings, and what you feel like you need to prove.

After you become adult, it more about responsibility, and less about you.

Being right is the least of our worries; shake back and lose the attitude.

If you have a point to prove, make a believer out of yourself; do something positive. Who cares about somebody that doubted you?!

That is not beneficial to us right now! The goal is to save as many lives as possible.

To take pride in our growth and become more responsible.

We must continue to uplift and improve the mental stability of our young people.

And if nothing else at all, we need to let go of our egos!

Love Is My Weakness

Dear Love,

I know this might sound crazy to you, but I'm open to being hurt again. Believe it or not, you are what I need.

And maybe one day soon we'll meet again.

It seems like ever since the first day that we met, my experiences haven't been the same.

It feels like I've experienced a whole new world without you.

I've tried looking for you, but I don't know where you are. I've tried calling you…

But I guess the number wasn't right. Or maybe you blocked me!

I've gone back to where we last seen each other; I was hoping you'd be there.

But no one's seen you around. I'm sick; I really wish I could talk to you.

You tried to explain so many things to me, but I was immature back then; I didn't listen.

I'm sorry for hurting you. Back then, times were different. Things were moving so fast; what was I supposed to do?

You know how I get; when my mind is focused on something, that's it!

I was chasing my goals; hopefully, you understand.

A lot of time has passed between us, and there are so many things that we need to discuss.

I can't wait to show you have much I've grown.

Most significantly, I can't wait to listen to you tell me about your new adventures.

After so many years of being ignorant, I can appreciate another perspective.

Before, I only cared about my own; but now I know why I needed yours.

There are valuable lessons that I can learn from you.

But until that time comes, I'll see you later...

Still loving you and missing you,

My Love!

Imagine This

Butterscotch chain choker, gift her with the herringbone
She not even the flashy type, but she knows how we get along
Matching wrist, matching kicks, I guess that's what we're lounging in
Pull up in that five, leave out in that six
Laidback in the rides, we ain't gotta touch shit
Got a butler and a maid; they help complement the trips
Not into alcohol, so its water we sip
Checking on these stocks, for our son and our daughter
Trying to set a great example, as the mother and the father
No rosary, just glory to me
When I met baby girl, she was royalty

Father God

You have given me discernment, and because of that, you continue to
inspire me.
You are my peace on a hectic day.

You are the solace that I seek, and my relaxation on a stormy night.
You are the wind that allows me to take a deep breath,
And the assurance to enjoy the fresh air.

In you, I seek favor and understanding.

Father, I come to you right now,
Knowing that you are already aware.

From the beginning to the ending, I seek vision and clarity.
Continuously, I am in search of a love,
hoping that it is fulfilling, and comparable to the gift.

Father, have your way with me.

Help me to be patient.
Equip me with the endurance and teach me how to hold on.

Help me to trust in your work wholeheartedly,
Confident that your plan is perfect for me.

In Jesus' name, I submit these prayers unto you...

Abba Father, Amen.

Questioning Day

7/27/21

I used to show love until you questioned my purpose
Now I gotta throw you in the box with the rest of the workers
I'm disappointed in you; how dare you question me
Challenging my existence, second-guessing my pedigree
Haven't you learned by now, don't you know how I get down
Everything I overcame, it still couldn't keep me down
Haven't I shown you before, the type of value that I hold
Can't you feel how I heat it up, whenever it gets cold
Ain't I consistent in my work
Did I not make my mother proud
Can't you see that I'm a big deal
It's a difference when I'm around
I bet if you look up to the heavens, you can see it's brighter now
I think I hear my father speaking
That's my son, with a smile

Lesson:

Closeness isn't always a good thing. In fact, it can sometimes be one of the most damaging parts of a relationship.

Friends, family, and associates alike, all of whom can sometimes be too close and too familiar, that they become a detriment to your growth patterns.

And at that instant, separation from what was becomes an imminent cause for change.

Control

Never get too close
They might call you clingy
Never overstay your welcome
They might say you are getting attached
Never tell them too much
Cause then they'll talk behind your back
And once you hear it in discussion
Someone says that you're not real
Become selective with your thought
And never tell them how you feel
They may start calling you emotional
To try and break the seal
But regardless of what they're saying
You always keep it chill
Say good morning and have a nice day
Then leave it right there

Special Delivery

They say I talk a lot,

But if you listen, then my mouth will stop,

Let me get it off my chest,

I'm trying to express myself,

So, if you're talking while I'm talking,

Then I have to talk over you,

The roof to the convertible, I got you covered,

Like gravy to a pork chop, I got you smothered,

I'm not that kind of meat, the one you eat with your hands,

I just deliver it so well, you gotta eat it out the pan,

I'm hot.

My Eyes Never Lie

As I struggle to sit before you

My knees begin to weaken

In the effort of trying to stand

I am not a fan of you

Nor am I a fan of your work

Because I am only a fan of my own

I'm only concerned with me

It's not that I don't like you

I just don't like what I see in you

A bogus imagination

A false depiction

That's not what I came to see

I used to be proud of you

In hopes that you would cheer for me

But now I'm ashamed of you

And all that has come to be

And it's not that I hate you

But the reality is

How much hate you have for me

Friendz

If you pay close enough attention, soon you will realize that there are a lot of part-time people in this world telling lies.

Some people only talk to you when it's structured around terms, but no one should have to be in the friendly company of a worm.

Be cautious of friendships that always make you wonder or question where you stand within the relationship.

Friendships are to be valued, sacred, and strong.

As friends, we should hold each other accountable for our actions, and then speak truth to empower one another.

For me,

I personally feel like it's a vital part of my relationships, that I celebrate the people around me.

I think it's very meaningful that you clap for your friends during their winning seasons in life.

While things may never be perfect in our relationship, it's still imperative that you play your position and stand solid within the relationship.

Some of the smartest people in relationships, they've learned to play in the background.

Because not only do they know their assignment, but they also recognize the responsibility that comes with the spotlight.

There is a huge benefit to mystery; there's nowhere to hide once the lights come on.

The strongest relationships understand the importance of loyalty.

Loyalty is a two-way street, and it should always be respected.

Lesson:

Life is one big journey, and it is full of ups and downs. And along that journey, there will be many roads of traveled paths. There is no harm in seeking inspiration. Furthermore, we all should want to feel inspired by someone, for there is true significance in valuing people who make you better.

Analyzing The Energy

Analyzing the mistakes of others is not the same as judging them.

You're the owner of your happiness; so, once you notice the changes, the ones that make you feel lonely and empty inside, that's when you've got to take notice.

At that moment, that's when you've got to realize that you aren't operating at your highest frequency.

Say it's my fault and take real ownership!

And then adjust yourself mentally, to make a full and complete change.

Granted, the circumstances that surround you may not be in your control.

But you do have control over your choices.

You chose how those things affect you mentally.

You have a choice of how you want to view things, both in a negative or positive light.

You also choose how you approach the next situation.

Life is a balancing act, but most notably, it's about learning from our lessons.

This is how we grow; onward and upward. Cheers to becoming better people.

Friends Of Mine

Inspired by Thomasina

Are like family
They don't get much closer than that

And I got a few to find
Posted on my wanted poster

Let's toast to the bonds, that I have with their kids
Cause Lord knows
I couldn't have imagined it, never fathom it
I promise that

Real friends are like enemies
They're always on your back
If you not handling your business
They're gonna double right back

That's the blessings of a friend tho
They're there when you need them
If you strugglin' and you're hungry
They're gonna be there just to feed you
With a plate or with a word

It'll be something that you needed
A blessing in disguise
Like, Mrs. Porter made pies
It's sweet on the lips

But it's wholesome for the soul
It's the therapy that you need
After they beat you down cold
It's the brother that you need
After a car repo

When you runnin' from your mother
And you need somewhere to go
A brother will open up
And lie to your mother at the door

That's a real friend
Or maybe just friends of mine

Better Days

Stay down until you come
Playgrounds, until they dug up
It took a lot to spend the night
But there never was no slumber
Party all night
And sleep is when the sun up
Talk about a wonder
Those were the years
We could move around the town
Back when we were the kids
We used to laugh and cry tears
We did it without a care
What happened to love that we shared around here
Three hots in a cot, pork and beans was a meal
Remember you had to eat your food before you left the chair
Blue magic was the grease on your box braided hair
And every year for Christmas
Got some brand-new underwear
Those were the days that we all miss and love
Thank God for those blessings, and the ones who gifted us

The Vessel

Part 1

Food, clothes, and shelter
A family that's not your own
Peace, love, and wisdom

A place where arguments are a normal thing

It's the joy of being accepted
A place where basketball and sports are always the top of discussion

The pleasure of feeling alive
To a part of something bigger than yourself

Family, bonds, and friendship
Good music, lots of laughter, and fun
Endless stories, talking about yesteryear and reminiscing about the good old days

Listening while learning the lessons for tomorrow

Grateful for the opportunity to be corrected by love
Fulfilled with understanding
And the disappointment when it all come to an end

Great times with good people, the extended family, and the ones you love

The Vessel

A Dose of Confidence

If your vision of purpose isn't crystal clear at this very moment,
Don't stress about it.
Because what is plainly obvious,
Is that you are here for a reason.
Divinity is something that none of us can escape,
There is designated purpose for your existence!

So instead of fighting and arguing about every detail,
Choose to live and be in love with life.
Embrace you,
Learn from the past and discontinue the ways of old.

Be a willing listener,
Compromise for future success.

Allow yourself to be flexible.
Open your mind to new possibilities,
Understanding that there are times when vulnerability is necessary...

As you continue to elevate,

Rely on your instincts.
Trust your spirit to expose what you can't see.
Your inner you won't lie to you,
Nor will it sell you short.

Have a dose of confidence!

A Letter to Grandma

(Ms. Lee)

I apologize, and I'm sorry!
I never got the chance to say my goodbyes, even though I don't believe in (saying goodbye). I still should have come and spoke my peace. I should have been strong enough, and wise enough to say thank you. All those nights, you let me sleep and eat what I wanted. For all those times you cared for me and shared your love. Whenever I was fighting in the park, and you never said a thing. I owed you for that! I was supposed to say thank you!

I was supposed to say thank you, for taking me in. I was supposed to give you time for being more than a friend. You would always listen to me when nobody did. I was supposed to say thank you, for treating me like I was one of your kids. For letting me sit and be mad at your kitchen table. I was supposed to say thank you, instead of being mad and ungrateful.

But my stubbornness, it got to me, indeed it held me back. It always did, and you knew that. I genuinely appreciated your love, and I needed you for that! But still, I was wrong. I never did say thank you!

A few nights before the funeral, maybe a day or two. Me and Jordan got into an argument. About what, who knows? But because I felt that he was closer to Kevin, I chose to stay at home. I talked to my mother about it, and she tried to convince me. But you know, it's something about me, I don't listen when I'm upset. So, she obliged, I chilled, and then we left it at that.

I asked her to write me a note. That was selfish of me!

I let my pride get in the way; there are no excuses for that.

So, Grandma, I apologize!

I hope it's not too late to say that… I am forever grateful; I love you, and I miss you dearly.

Appreciation

When I was lost in the wilderness,
You were my lifeline.
You helped me find my way home,
I admired your spirit.
As a friend and a confidant,
I was compelled by your commitment.
Your compassion to serve,
I was blessed to be a witness...
The love that you have for others,
It's been a blessing to see!
You've warmed my heart from a distance,
So affectionately...

It's so sad to see,
Me and you, we ain't speaking.
No more calls on the phones,
We ain't laughing on the weekends.
I guess it's quite bizarre, when referring to the gift,
Once you take it for granted,
Take a blink, and then you miss it...

L.Y.F.E.

(Live Young Free and Easy)

Part 1

Before I finally realized what happened, it was 17 years later, and I was still reliving every moment of my past.

All that hurt, disappointment, the trauma, and the pain.

The feeling of betrayal cost me.
I hadn't healed yet. I was still pointing the finger.
And I never took full control of my life.

And although our separation as brothers happened years ago.

The other side had moved on.

And anytime a discussion came up about what happened between us, the other side always found a way to place blame. And somehow, I became the victim.

And while life progressively moved on around me.
I found myself being stuck at 16, still expecting a conversation, and an apology to go along with it.

But it hasn't happened... And at this point, I don't expect it will.

And I'm okay with that.

So much for thinking, right...?

Self-preservation, it's life

Live Young, Free and Easy

A Different Type of Energy

I can't deal with certain people
It's so hard for me to sleep
I be waking up in cold sweats
Cramping in the sheets
When I pick up my phone
I gotta block and then delete
That's my number one go to
When I'm trying to find peace
Sometimes it be on them
Other times it's on me
Sometimes I need some space
When I'm trying to find me

L.Y.F.E (2)

(Live Young Free and Easy)

With you or without you, life moves on!

And as much as you want some people to say, hey, I'm sorry, I was wrong, or I apologize for hurting you.

For some people, it's not a part of their make-up. And perhaps not even in their DNA.

And for those stubborn individuals who are in denial, it's just not who they are.

You could go years atop of years, and you may never get the apology that you expect.

So, stop waiting for it!
For your sake…
It's worth it that you find time to heal.

Because it's your life, and anyone that loves you depends on you finding peace within it!

Life Cycle

Life isn't about taking the easy route or figuring out how to lighten the load as you navigate its terrain.

Life is a beautiful journey; it's about learning lessons and gathering information.

Life is about sacrifice and teaching, experiencing new environments, and gaining knowledge while you explore.

Every situation in life brings about a new degree of lessons. Either it teaches you to become something, or you are teaching someone else how to evolve into something.

Life is about breaking down and building up.

While there are many barriers that need to be broken down, there are also numerous changes that need to take place, so that life doesn't become stagnant.

This is what the cycle of life is all about; growth and elevation, creating and recreating again.

Thankful Prayer

Dear Heavenly Father,

I come to you right now, and I just want to say thank you. Thank you for freedom. Thank you for an open mind and a loving heart. Thank you for the angels that you send to help guide and protect us when we are lost and in need in the wilderness.
Thank you, Father, for your love (agape).

Thank you for the loved ones who have been given second chances and new opportunities. Thank you for friendship. Thank you for the many prayers that we often don't hear, but somebody cared enough to pray for us!

Father, I call out to you for those who would also like to call out to you, but they are afraid and don't know how. Lord, I stand in the gap for them, the lost souls who have a need and a desire to want to know you. Father God, I thank you again and again for all the grace and mercy that you've shown to a sinner like me.

Lord, I can't thank you enough for the gift of living, for life has given us all so many blessings; we are extremely fortunate of everything we have been given.

Lord, I just want to honor you and give you all the praise.

Abba Father, Amen.

Thoughts of a Sinner

If everyone is a sinner

Where does all of the judgment come from

How are you calling me a devil, after all of the shit you've done

And I'm not calling you a hater, because I'm just like you

And you can't call me a hypocrite; I criticize myself too

So, all that talking at me, scrap it, pappy

Cause I really ain't hearing it, Point, Blank, and Period

It's really that serious, as simple as it gets

I speak on how I feel, and I say it from my chest

A notch above the rest, best I do with the best

Never settle for less, even though they try to sell me on

I guess they think it all game, but I bet my family on it

You can take nothing from me, that I ain't willing to give

And I ain't giving up now, so we all fighting to live

Only losers don't prosper; we winning the whole Oscar

Don't care about you judging me; I'm living like a mobster

I'm rewriting the rules, and creating my own lane

You can't subject me to criticism; I'm doing my own thang

The Truth About Me

I got to be transparent cause I really don't want to see you

When God show me signs, I need to separate from people

Can't sit around complaining, cause then I start to turn evil

It's like an eye for an eye, or a needle for a needle

I spray repellent on me, so that trash don't seep through

I don't want you anywhere around me, and I don't care that we not people

Treat you like an old toy; I love you, then I leave you

Leave that old shit in the past; I don't really think I need you

It's time to be my own man, and you and me not equal

As a matter of fact, let's just end this now

I'll see you when I see you, let's stop messing around

Uncut Clarity

I can see the bullshit from a mile away up here,
Only God, I fear, I don't need your cheers
I won't be sitting at the bar, ordering a round of beer
I could care less about opinions, or how none of y'all feel
I'm about to do what I do, and get gone from here
I've grown from here; I don't belong around here
I done see people fall and stay home around here
Played bones around here, they shot chrome around here
This don't even feel the same; this ain't home around here

Too Many Hands In

Everyone in your life has a distinct hand in the pot
Some people come as a helping hand,
And consequently, others are there to destroy
Some come to fix, tighten, and build,
While there are a select few
They only want to loosen and see things fall through
The essential task is learning who is who,
And why they are there
Recognizing what motives are pure and which ones are faulty
Time, space, and absence,
Is the perfect occasion for an opportunist,
To show traits in rare form

Good People

Good words are like nectar, sweet like honey,

Warm like the sun's rays, when it's hot out and sunny,

Cool like the wind's breeze, when it's 40 degrees,

Good til' the last drop, so good, it's too good,

Too much to make you stop,

But when it's gone, it's gone; you can't order another round.

Lesson:

People with good intentions say a lot of informative stuff. It's up to you to grasp the message and keep it close.

Because the longer it takes you to get a taste, once you realize how good it was, it's gone.

And by then, it's too late. There are no second servings.

You missed out!

Good Morning Prayer

May the love of God shine bright on your dreams today!

May your prayers be attached to his will,
May you be provided with increase so big that you smile from ear to ear.

As you have been awakened today, give honor and thanks.
May his mercy offer blessings upon you and grant you with a fresh start.
No worries, no tears, and no sorrows.

Father, I pray that you eliminate the heartache and pain
If only for one day, give us peace.

I ask that your love be welcomed as a refresher to the mind,
And of the spirit.

In these things, we pray,

Abba Father, Amen.

Don't Pity Me

Fuck a dollar and a dream

I want a whole million more

40 acres ain't enough

I came to settle the score

Thought I grew up poor

I used to knock on John's door

Asking neighbors for their bottles

Never met my role model

Never knew him

Never saw him

Never knew who he was

My father died when I was young

His spirit floating above

I was ignorant to life, misguided with no direction

A deviant to my mother, and a lost adolescent

Fallen Isn't Failed

Just because you've fallen, that doesn't mean you've failed.
You could've done yourself better by not accomplishing your goal.
Fallen just simply means that you slipped,
You lost your footing somewhere.

And that's okay!

Everyone has a slip or two.
Everybody of importance has lost some ground,
They, too, have had to make up or readjust their focus.

Fallen isn't failed.
It simply means that you've moved from one level to the next.

Taking a step back can be a good thing.
Sometimes we're moving too fast, and we are gaining too much too quickly.
Often, we aren't ready for what's next.

Taking a step back gives you the time and opportunity,
To re-evaluate yourself,
To re-think your approach,
And make plans for a new situation.

Lesson:
Fallen does not equal failed... Success has its own formula. Create it,
Sample it, Test it, Approve it.

Everybody Ate

Once I eat, then I ate,

And then everybody straight,

I ain't gotta waste time, trying to fill another plate,

And I didn't get it back then, but now I understand it perfectly,

I take this personally, the position I'm in,

Because I talk so much, people think I don't listen,

But my eyes wide shut, I can see with clearer vision,

It only takes me; I'm a man on a mission,

To see all that I need to see, and be who I be,

Preparation over everything, I spit it like a prequel,

Follow up back-to-back, just like a sequel,

My study game crazy, and the action part is lethal,

I'm sticking to myself, can't put trust in other people,

And if I can't trust you now, then I don't need you around,

And I ain't actin' funny, I'm just speaking to you spiritually,

Because the ones who really love me, they gonna let me be me,

I done helped plenty eat, but still, they act like they didn't need me,

So, when it's time to fill this plate,

Just know I gotta eat greedy.

Grace Is Sufficient

You have been forgiven because Christ has forgiven me,

No longer am I choosing to dwell in a broken place,

I have prayed, and I have released the evil energy

That energy that has caused my anger toward you,

Today I have forgiven you, for wanting to listen,

For having the humble mind and a spirit to say I'm sorry,

To recognize and accept your responsibility is powerful,

That means a lot to me.

However, I still need to inform you,

Even though I have freed myself of the anger that I once held close,

That doesn't mean that I will forget as quickly as I forgave you,

The scars and the wounds still exist,

The pain often returns whenever the weather changes,

Almost like changing the tires on an old ride,

I'm back riding fresh, in that same old shit,

I think you're starting to get my drift,

We can change the shit, clean it up,

But there's still that stench,

The odors' still there, can't you smell in the air,

I know it's not fair, but that's just the way it is,

I'm so appreciative of Grace, thank God that he forgave you,

The same way as he continues to forgive me.

Family Ties

I never had a happy home; that why I needed yours
Always valued was you taught, so I explored for more
Argument in the living room, put circles on the wall
So much food was on the table, I wanted it all
My discovery was truth, with even your flaws
That was critical for me; I needed the love
Both the mental and the spiritual
It was more than enough

Discernment

(I Know Me)

There are no strangers in my house
Because I don't want them here physically
Despite my interactions
Personalities aren't enough for me
Anxiety and confusion, it's a lot not to trust
Conflict mixed with anger; I'm overwhelmed by is mentally
I keep my space sacred, so I can talk to God religiously

Forgiveness

A cheerful giver,
But kindhearted and angry.

I'm sick and tired of it,
All I hear is complaining.

To be honest with you,
I'd ride alongside of you,
I'd put my pride to the side,
And go stride for stride with you.

I'd sacrifice my time, or even my life for you.

But only if I knew that you would be responsible too.

If not, then tell me why I should sit around and wait for you?

Tell me why it's my fault, that you aren't where you're supposed to be?

Tell me why you're complaining and not living your life free?

Tell me what's the reason, that I should sacrifice for you?

Can you please explain to me, why I need to accommodate you?

I'm Sorry

I'm sorry if I ever hurt you,
Or said something that rubbed you the wrong way.

I'm sorry if I disregarded your feelings,
I wasn't being purposeful.

I apologize for the disrespect,
And if you feel that I neglected you,

I apologize for the hurt,
And anytime I have ignored you.

For anything that I have done to you,
Please forgive me for it all...

I apologize for your pain,
Or any harm that I caused.

I apologize for being careless,
And reckless with my words.

I apologize for my actions,
And my mistakes too.

I apologize if I was unfaithful,
And for my betrayal too.

Please forgive me for that,
Forever I'm grateful.

I'm Sorry!

If You Love Me

What if when you asked me those questions,
And my response was that I didn't know,
Would you assume I was lying to you?
Or would you suggest that something was wrong,

What if I judged you, based on the flaws that I saw in you?
Do you think I would look at you differently?
And if I did, would I be wrong?

Or would you start to think less of me?

Realistically speaking,
If we all were perfect,

Then there would be no reason for Christ's salvation.

If we were all perfect,

Then there would be no reading for God's Grace and Mercy.

Therefore, my only pledge is this:

If you love me, please tell me now,
Treat me like the ice cream on your cone, that you catch before it hits
the ground.

If you love me, please tell me now,

Because tomorrow's gonna come and I might not be around.

If you love, please tell me now,

You don't wanna wait until I'm gone, or I'm six feet in the ground.

If you love me, this is how you show me how,

Greet me with a handshake, a hug,

And please show me your smile,

If you love me, please tell me now.

Dear America

I hope you hear me,
Please don't make me a martyr!

Let my legacy stand for more than just painted pictures and created murals of me.

While I'm here, let me breathe. Let me enjoy my family.
Let me enjoy my life. Let me live on this earth for as long as the good Lord allows me to.

I don't want to die in vain. Nah, I don't want that.
If you truly love me, honor, and respect me.
Just let me live.

Lord knows, when it's my time to go, I won't need your sympathy; they'll be no reason to light candles and sing old songs about how much you miss me.

Because I lived!

My purpose on this earth is far greater than that, broken hearts, and tragedy.
No, it's far more impactful than that; a bunch of tears and sad songs, or compounded letters that make upwards on a tee shirt.

I am more than just some image to be posted on the internet.

My calling is to live with great intention. I have been called and created to do more, to be more.

So please, America, let me live.

Thank you.

LESSONS, RHYMES, POEMS AND PRAYERS

SPONSORS

Made in the USA
Monee, IL
26 April 2022